Published by Mosedale Publishing
mosedalepublishing@gmail.com

Cover art: Martine Collister
Illustrations: Jack Collister Brown

ISBN paperback 978-1-7385158-0-6
ISBN e-book 978-1-7385158-1-3

Fingling the Snargle

A Memoir

Sarah Mosedale

For Martine

For all our stories

Contents

LET'S START HERE

Health & Safety

I'm starting to believe my own stories. I hope you won't. Everything here is deniable, non-litigious, unattributed. All sources are suspect. All names have been redacted. Any resemblance to any person you think you know or may once have known is entirely coincidental. If you think that little town in the far north sounds like X that's just your opinion. If you think you recognise my surname, I assure you, you are mistaken. Every word is a lie. Every other word is a lie. Some paragraphs are true, others are not. Choose one. Then choose another. You're still not right.

You follow me down the rabbit hole at your own risk. We are all underinsured. There are no refunds.

The First Time

The first time is the worst time.

I was to go mad several times in my thirties and forties but each time, no matter how terrifying the situation, there was a part of me, no matter how tiny, that knew this had happened before. And that helped.

The first time there was no help.

Try and imagine it. Try hard.

You are in your best friend's kitchen, her two toddler sons are playing, her man is out at work. It's a sunny day. Everything is bright and crystal clear, edges so sharp they're murderous. Every object is charged with an awful meaning just beyond your grasp. Something terrible is about to happen but nobody else seems to know.

You realise there is no air in the room. It's very important to explain this. You demonstrate, grasping at the space and opening your hands to show they are empty. You shout. Your friend knows something about dealing with hysteria and slaps you lightly across the face. It's nothing.

Then the full horror hits you. When all the air is gone everyone's body will explode. You look at your hands, you can see them starting to go red and swell. Every single person on the planet will die. Everyone. It's the end of the human race. It's the end of millennia of evolution. No one will survive. The human race is finished. It's over.

And it's your fault.

You did it. You pulled the plug on the atmosphere. Something anyone could have done but nobody did. You did it. You killed every human being on earth.

How do you feel now?

I'm on the floor screaming. An unearthly sound. The next door neighbour leaps to peer over the fence. My friend runs to the phone. *Ambulance! Now!*

The rest of that day is fragments.

I'm looking out the back door of the ambulance, somehow calmer at this point. My sister has arrived and is with me. My friend is standing in her front garden holding her younger son. He wants to wave goodbye to the ambulance. I am stunned by her bravery. She must know death is imminent but is kind, gentle, putting his needs first. I loathe myself for my cowardice.

I am in the waiting room at the hospital. I am running from person to person. I am begging them to kill me. They cannot meet my eyes. They cannot help me. I am apologising for my behaviour.

I am face down on a high bed. There are people around me, they are speaking gently, I am doing what I am told, they are pulling my trousers down, they are injecting me.

I am lying on a mattress on the floor in the same room. I have a blanket over me. My sister is sitting on a chair. They have given her a cup of tea. Time has passed and I can see she is still alive. I am slowly realising the world isn't ending. I check this with my sister. She agrees.

I feel some relief. This is a good thing. But I am already embarrassed. And anxious. What happens next? How do I claw myself back from here?

FALLING FROM THE APPLE TREE

Grandfather and the Bird

Once upon a time, a little girl of six or seven years was walking up a steep tree-lined hill with her grandfather. It was a special day for the little girl because her grandfather lived far away and did not often visit. It was a Sunday and the two of them were returning home from church. That was special too. Her family never went to church.

The little girl knew her parents did not believe in god and, because her parents were still godlike to her, it followed that they were right. Jesus was a nice story maybe - though bits were troubling - but obviously not true. The little girl loved stories of all kinds but she knew how to tell the difference between ones that were true and ones that were made up. It seemed odd to her that some grownups believed the Jesus story. All that walking on water and raising the dead and everything.

No one else wanted to go to church with her grandfather; even her grandmother preferred to stay at home. So the little girl asked if she could go. Why? I was that little girl and I cannot tell you truthfully. It was a long time ago.

Maybe she wanted to spend some time with her grandfather, a man of few words. Maybe she was curious about church and this was a way to get a look inside. Maybe she hoped her grandfather would be pleased. It was obvious from the way her father treated him that he was a very important person. It's even possible she wanted to score points against her younger brother. If that is true, she would have done her best to forget it.

But I suspect she told herself she was being kind, that her grandfather would be sad if he was on his own. That little girl wanted to like herself very much and she tried hard to do so. I wish I could tell her she didn't need to try so hard. I wish I could tell her it would get easier but warn her it would be a long struggle. I wish I could tell her I love her. I suppose I'm telling her now.

There they are, the two of them, walking up that steep hill. Maybe she's chattering and he's grunting acknowledgement. Maybe he's singing to her; he used to do that sometimes. But I doubt it. The hill is very steep and he's old. She's quite a tubby little girl, not sporty, so she's probably not got much breath to spare either. So I imagine them climbing in a companionable silence.

Suddenly the grandfather stops, making a sound of disgust. She turns to find him searching for a handkerchief to wipe away what has just landed on his dark coat.

Bird poo!

She is shocked. Her world is tumbling around her. If a bird can do this to her grandfather – if he has so little power - what does that say about her parents? About Jesus? About everything?

Being an Atomicker

It was our fault. Like so much was. Our English teacher wouldn't tolerate chewing gum, she had a nose for it; prowling round the classroom sniffing, she inevitably tracked down the culprit.

There was nae chewing gum here till the Atomickers came.

None of us dared call bullshit, Granny G was stooped, ancient - and anyway, we liked her. A little ball of wrinkly, laughing-eyed provocation, looking up at us through thick lenses, from under her grey bun. She wasn't one for punishment - her obvious distress shame enough for any perpetrator.

Her other obsession was with the correct enunciation of the word 'yes'. It drove her crazy whenever anyone said yeah. Which we did a lot. It was hard to change that habit and 'yes' sounded so formal. One day she was reading to us from a modern novel. When one of the characters said yeah she rendered it as a contemptuous snarl, making no sense in the context. Silent eye contact, grins and raised eyebrows flashed around the room. She couldn't recognise the word written down! The world was changing around Granny G and we Atomickers weren't the half of it.

Though it was undeniable that we'd brought seismic changes when we'd flooded in ten years ago. Her tiny isolated town, once supported by fishing and the production of Caithness flagstone, was now surrounded by our housing estates, population swollen times five. We'd come from all over Scotland and even, like my family, from the ancient enemy, England. Our fathers were scientists, engineers, skilled craftsmen; their pay packets bigger, coming like clockwork every month.

But the middle class attributes that might have been expected to smooth our paths were precisely what damned us here. I realise now I was lucky to be catchment-areaed into the most mixed of the three primary schools - the one that many of the locals attended. They were the ones with the history, the culture, the connection to the wild, beautiful, dangerous landscape of sea, peat bog, cliff. We were the incomers, rootless, adrift; if we fancied ourselves the elite we were sorely mistaken.

Of course I exaggerate. Many locals had decent jobs at the power station, many incomer families struggled with low pay, many lasting friendships and romances crossed the line. But the line was real. My brother, born in situ unlike me, hung out mainly with locals and developed a proper accent, one of several accents I learned to slip in and out of without thinking. (My father, passing by in the hall, could always tell which friend was on the other end of the line.) I competed ferociously at school, my brother didn't; he thought I was a snob, I worried he might be right.

I continued chewing gum and saying yeah but I tried not to do either in Granny G's class.

Glorious Everyday Surroundings

How do you cordon off a beach? I mean a whole beach, not just a bit where they find a body. A whole beach. Like, notices saying you cannot swim in the sea, you cannot walk on the sand. It is very dangerous. Particles. Do not cross the dunes to get to this beach. Go away. Go away altogether and do something else. Forget about this bay; it is no good any more. It might not be any good for thousands of years.

She didn't go there to find out. But she bet other people did. And she bet they walked on the sand. Though they probably didn't go in the sea. The sea was freezing. Except, everyone said, that bit near the outlet pipes. That bit was warm, tropical fish swam there. She wondered how the fish got there. How they survived the journey. Maybe every part of the ocean had the potential to create tropical fish, fish generated from rock and reef, sand and surf, when the conditions were right. What kind of fish would emerge here? Fish that glowed in the dark? Fish with long half-lives? Fish that looked at you the wrong way, fish that knew too much. Loose-lipped, blabber-mouthed fish.

She remembered the day she'd walked on a different beach with a girl she knew, the beach you could get to from her house in eight minutes even walking slow. They'd been talking, oblivious to their glorious everyday surroundings, the bay with its headlands framing the perfectly presented island, just wandering along when suddenly the other girl had gasped and stopped dead. She'd looked down. They were surrounded by crabs. Crabs as far as the eye could see and big ones too, not cute babies, big ones that could give you a hell of a bite. Horrified, they'd ran, scrambling over the shingle, big smooth stones that could break your ankle easy, to reach the safety of the walkway.

They'd been near the crab factory right enough. An undemonstrative single-story building, white pebble dashed against the gales like their houses were. Not like the experimental nuclear power station ten miles away, its golf ball reactor a global icon.

When she'd thought about it afterwards it struck her that none of the crabs had been moving. The other girl reckoned they were dead, empty shells, crab factory discards that had somehow ended up in the wrong place. She wasn't so sure. She'd felt her stomach clench, her breath come short.

The Thief

Could you come up to the office please?

It's nearing the end of your first day in your first Saturday job. And it's gone well, you've been polite and helpful, the customers have been friendly whether or not they've recognised you - it's a small town - and the till has been easy to work.

Sure. With your best stab at an assistant's smile.

You follow the owner up the narrow stairs at the back of the shop and into a small room. He looks at you. He looks serious. You adopt a polite expectant expression and wait for him to speak. You imagine that he wants to make some positive comment on your work, maybe to ask if you have any questions.

We like to be able to trust our girls.

You still don't get it. You nod and smile, maintain the look, wait for him to continue. His statement seems obvious, no answer required.

Then he drops his bombshell. He saw you. He saw you sell a girl you know from school a packet of cigarettes for a ha'penny. Your mouth falls open. You hadn't. You didn't. You sold her a ha'penny packet of chewing gum.

But he saw you. He's sorry but there's no point arguing. He saw you. He's starting to look embarrassed. You're not following the script. This is where you're supposed to give it up. This is where you're supposed to realise you can't contradict the evidence of his own eyes. Oh yes, he's assured you, it was through his very own eyes that he saw you do it.

But you persist. Because you didn't.

He is adamant you did. He saw you. There's nothing else to say, yet, unforgivably, you continue saying things. You can see the distaste creeping across his face; your refusal to accept the truth damning you in his eyes moment by moment. One thing to steal some cigarettes for a friend - unacceptable of course, perhaps even reprehensible, certainly a sackable offence, but the sort of mistake a naive young girl might make. Quite another to lack even the self-respect to recognise when the game is up, to keep digging in, to persist in this unseemly charade.

You should be slinking away by now; if you can't manage that you should be flouncing out, performing offence, storming off in high teenage dudgeon. But you're not doing either of those things. You're standing there like a great lump, tears in your eyes, insisting black is white, cigarettes are chewing gum, telling him he didn't see what he saw. He's a patient man but you're pushing it. All he wants now is to get you out of his shop, to forget he ever hired you.

You make that difficult for him. You leave but you go straight round to that girl's house, you tell her what's happened, she gets her dad. Her dad is sweet, he listens to you both, he hears your distress, your outrage.

He says, *I'm only going to ask this once. Did you do it?*

You both swear you didn't. You tell him you're not saying it's impossible you would ever do such a thing, you're not claiming you're better than that. But you didn't. He takes you at your word. It's such heaven to be believed. When you're telling the truth.

Your dad comes on board too, no problem. The dads talk. The mums play no part, this is men's business. The owner agrees to a meeting at your house but he makes it clear it's pointless, he saw what he saw. His wife comes with him. She seems nice, you tell her that her husband has made a mistake. The chewing gum is on the back wall near the cigarettes and both packets are white, though of different sizes. He saw you hand over the chewing gum, he wrongly thought it was a packet of cigarettes. That is what happened. She tells you her husband is a good man but he is convinced about what he saw and he is not the kind of man who would ever change his mind.

And she is right about that. The dads talk about solicitors, he doesn't care. He knows very well they're bluffing, you're fourteen, it's a Saturday job. He tells them to go ahead. He knows what he saw.

You get a Saturday job at Woolworth's.

Such A Relief

At last! An explanation for why her mum has turned into a mindless zombie, a zombie with terrifying empty eyes who only says things like *Did you have a nice day at school?* in an expressionless voice like a machine. A machine with no interest whatsoever in the answer. A nightmare mum in a dream she never wakes up from however much she shouts and cries. A mum who has stopped even pretending to love her.

And it's such a simple problem! Her mum drinks too much. Obvious solution - her mum needs to stop drinking. Such a relief. If only all problems were so easy to solve. She's fifteen, very capable, she knows she can help with this. More than happy to spend a bit more time with her mum; she accepts she's been a bit thoughtless perhaps, treats the place like a hotel, always out with her friends. She and her mum used to get on so well, now she knows what needs to change she's keen to get started. Maybe her mum would like to play tennis or go swimming? It'll be great to get back to the chats they used to have.

She remembers her real mum fondly, with pride. She was a mum you could talk to, a mum who treated you and your friends like people, not nuisances like some of the other mums did. She was different in other ways too - glamorous, always well made up, hair styled, interested in clothes, modern-looking. There's a photo of her walking down the high street, pushing the baby's big pram; in her 1950s headscarf she looks chic, perky, like a film star. Like Princess Margaret but younger, much more beautiful. Clever too - got a French degree. Not much interested in cooking - not like her best friend's mum with her wonderful baking - but convenience foods are coming in.

She explains her plans to her mum. Stopping drinking, doing things together, good chats. Her mum finds some dregs of emotion. Enough to make it clear that she is being ridiculous. Drinking, what drinking? Problem, what problem? She cries. Her mum is not remotely interested.

She demands that her dad do something. He is the other adult in the house after all. Her dad consults books, the GP. It turns out he's been prescribing Valium for years. Apparently nothing can be done until her mum accepts she has a problem and wants to do something about it. Her dad, a scientist, decides to prove that she has a problem. They took up brewing their own beer years ago, his wife does it all now. He starts to keep a daily log of the bottles, numbers full, numbers empty. He draws up tables, graphs. He discovers she is averaging eight pints a day. He shows her the results of his research. She is not remotely interested. Drinking, what drinking? Problem, what problem?

The dad is a positivist. He believes he has demonstrated the problem exists. He cannot understand how his wife can look at his data and maintain that she does not have a problem. In fact she does have a problem, but it is very different from what he imagines. Her problem is that her husband and daughter are threatening her drinking.

She will go on to defend her drinking almost to the death. She will defend it long past beer brewing being forbidden - she will swap to buying whisky. She will defend it long past her children tipping that down the sink, screaming at her, begging her to stop. She will defend it long past stopping eating, long past being thrown out of the marital home, long past drying out on psych wards that pull her back from the edge only to give her the strength to buy another bottle, long past begging on the London streets outside the off licence in her nightie. She will defend it past the medics telling the family she will certainly drink herself to death, that there is no hope.

One by one her family abandon her. Even the daughter finally accepts that she must choose between herself and her mother. Finally accepts that she cannot make her mum stop drinking, that turning up once a week with bags of food is not helpful. That the choice is whether she goes down with her mother or lets her drown alone in that sweet and deadly amber flood.

She chooses to let her go down alone. Over the next two years she steels herself for the phone call informing her of her mother's death. A phone call that never comes.

The Washing

How do you do it?

My mother, having no washing machine, did everything by hand. I am standing beside her at the kitchen sink. Tightly wrung out towels and sheets lie like thick grey twisted snakes on the draining board. I couldn't really have seen them from that angle, I was too small. But I was there and she was there and they were there. Of those three facts I am sure.

I don't remember anything else about the washing for several years. Probably because I was at school and had no interest in what was happening at home while I wasn't there. I do remember that by the age of thirteen I was doing my own washing. I don't remember why. Maybe my clothes weren't being washed quickly enough. I didn't have a lot of clothes. Maybe I got tired of pestering my mother and decided to do it myself.

I scrubbed my knickers and tights every evening in the hand basin, using the bar of Imperial Leather that was never replaced until the soap was a sliver of memory on the back of the red label. Hung them on the towel rack over the bath. I washed my other clothes with soap powder in the small sink in our downstairs bathroom. From there, once well wrung out, they could be whipped through the kitchen, out the back door and onto the line.

Eventually, with bad grace, my father started driving to the laundrette. I'm pretty sure I declined any offer to take my washing. I don't remember this but it would make sense. I had the situation under control. And it was obvious he didn't want to do it.

Now I'm twenty, discharged from the psych ward back into my father's care. Having washed his hands of his dysfunctional wife, he has moved in his much younger girlfriend. She is wrestling with her twin tub. I have never seen one before and am rather horrified at the amount of physical effort involved in heaving the entire soaking load from one compartment to the other. I continue quietly washing my things in the downstairs bathroom while planning my suicide.

I tell my father that my mother used to spend hours doing the washing in the kitchen sink when I was a child. It seems this is news to him. Maybe he also had little interest in what went on in the house when he wasn't there. Avoiding my eye, he says she never asked for a washing machine. I say maybe she never imagined she could have one.

I fail to kill myself; instead I escape from home again but I never buy myself a washing machine. Friends think I'm crazy but I like washing my clothes by hand. I wash them in small batches, in a plastic basin, bending over the bath. It does take some physical effort but that feels good. After I do a batch of washing I feel like I am in control.

Much later, when we move my father into a care home, I take his fully automatic washing machine.

Bruv

I am standing in a room on the day of my mother's funeral and I am about to leave. We've all just returned from the crematorium. Except my brother. He didn't come because he fell into a rage over a radio being turned off before we left. Sitting, he looks sheepish but meets my eye. He and I have been through so much. Looking at him I feel very aware that I may never see him again. It's one of those rare moments whose huge significance we apprehend in real time. Something is drowning. Something is flashing past me at impossible speed in that moment in that dusty room.

I am completely unaware of anyone else present. All I can see is my brother. Snapshots down the ages. That cute little boy in his school blazer and shorts, three years my junior. Here he is again, crying snotty faced, holding my hand, me smirking, parents oblivious. And now a teenager, no longer cute, thin faced, hair clipped to a number two, apprentice bovver boy. He's got his own friends; my parents no longer pester me to let him tag along.

Now he's fifteen, just got out of prison, deeply shocked and friendless. I do my sister of mercy act, introducing him to the cool dope-smoking freaks I know. He turns on, tunes in and, for a while, calms down, seems happier and less angry. Later, when I get out of the psych ward, he is there again, also desperately unhappy and back in our dad's house. We suffer in a reasonable facsimile of solidarity, smoking rerolled cigarette butts till the early hours, dry eyed in front of the fire, dad berating us next day for wasting gas.

I escape to London, I help him escape too. We hit the squatting movement, I survive, he does less well. He bites the hand that feeds him, over and over again; he can't seem to tell the difference between friend and foe. We all exist only to be exploited, to be ripped off, it doesn't matter how little we have or how fairly we try to share it. Our mother, she of today's funeral, hangs in the longest. But eventually she makes the hardest choice of all and closes her door to him. I remember her crying, imagining him sleeping under a bridge outside in the cold. Terrible exclusions run in our family, we did it to her ages ago when her alcoholism turned her into a witch.

Years later my brother reappears, prodigal son-like, reformed by the love of a good woman and we all try again. It works well enough for several years. Then it doesn't. My mother copes, eventually dies. I live two hundred miles away. I only see him when I visit my mother. I won't be doing that again.

The Final Copy Edit

Time was I knew all them little twiddles. The one that means ‘insert here’ or ‘delete and replace with’, that says ‘change to a capital letter’ or ‘whoops sorry, my mistake, as you were’. I never was a proper copy editor, it was always just part of a job. I liked it though; I went on a two day training course and I had the manuals and the industry standard guide. I still do.

My mum loved editing too. But she did become a proper editor, the editor of the Hackney Pensioners' Press, a newspaper created by a group of local people, mostly Afro-Caribbean women. The focus was on campaigning and activism, although mum did eventually bow to pressure and include a much loathed (by her) poetry corner. As well as a symmetric crossword – which, as a frequent finisher of the Guardian cryptic, she enjoyed learning how to create.

We used to do the Guardian cryptic together on cosy Sunday afternoons in her flat, the three of us, after she'd taught me and my girlfriend the basics. Discussing different lines of attack, poring over the dictionary, trying out first this idea, then that, till a solution manifested itself – sometimes edging into view, letter by letter, sometimes crashing through the brain barrier in one blinding moment.

Anyway, editing, yes, we both enjoyed editing. And writing of course. But also very much the paring down, the punctuating, the triumphant moment when a superfluous word reveals itself and is purged, the pleasure of making a whole sentence redundant by a carefully placed and much shorter subordinate clause. The good feeling when a clumsy sentence metamorphoses into something smoother, something with rhythm, something with soul. And always one more typo somewhere to spot and slay.

One of the very last things I did for my mum was to copy edit the plaque on her coffin. The undertaker was embarrassed when I pointed out that her middle name was not May. Fortunately we were in the funeral parlour at the time so the error could be corrected. I only wish the final version could have been a copy edit with that little upward inflection showing precisely where the missing 'r' should be placed.

Mum would've loved it.

A Letter From Mum

This is your mum. Yeah, surprising I know. You lot are so clueless about death. Seems strange from here, really it does. Oh and just to clarify - we're not talking angels and harps. I was right about that. Load of crap.

It's been tough reading your stuff. We never talked about what it was like for you, did we? You hurt me too of course. No amount of whisky could blot out the memory of that terrible day you told me you would never see me again. Me sitting on the concrete walkway outside your Hackney Council flat banging on the door more and more weakly as the afternoon ground on. You inside with the stereo turned up full.

Me getting next door to knock on, *This lady says she's your mother?*

You, *Yeah she is but I don't want to see her any more.* Politely, shutting the door.

Couldn't believe you could be that hard. Didn't see you again for years.

I remember, much later, long after I'd stopped drinking and started living again and we were friends, in a sudden fit of grumpiness I spit out some hurt about that day.

You said, *Fine, we can talk about that if you want. But, if we do, we also have to talk about what it's like to be fifteen and find out your mum doesn't love you any more.*

That just killed me. There was no way I could bear to hear that. So we never talked about what we had done to each other.

I don't regret that. I hope you don't. We talked about lots of other stuff. I talked for years about your father, about his neglect, about how being a 1950s housewife destroyed me. It was the 1980s and you were a feminist so you heard me. Though it hurt again when eventually you said you'd heard enough about what a bastard he was. That he was your dad and you loved him and that if I needed to unload any more I should find myself a counsellor. But that's you - kind and accommodating up to a point and then utterly ruthless in pursuing your own self-interest. I suppose we're not that different. And I am glad that, against all the odds, your dad and I were able to be friends later.

You and I had such good times, didn't we? Those Greek islands... I hadn't been abroad since my university placement in Paris. Took some persuading, didn't I? My arthritis was pretty bad by then; I remember worrying there'd be nowhere to sit down. And your reply - *Oh yeah, right, that's a problem... there won't be any seats. Greek people don't sit down, do they?* But your teasing was gentle and you persisted until I overcame my fears.

God, it was great. I'll never forget the first time we got off the plane. The colours, the scents, the dry heat! It was like straight back to my Indian childhood. That package holiday was luxury I'd never imagined I'd see again. Me - sun bathing on beach loungers, paddling in the Med, enjoying heavenly food in seaside tavernas every night, completely uninterested in your retsina. Me! After that first holiday I swore I could die now, it would all have been worth it. We had at least six or seven...

I love you and I know you love me. Who would ever have thought we could get back to this place after everything that happened? But we did.

Forever

Your mum

Where's My Sister?

When we moved house my two-year-old sister started pulling her hair out, strand by strand. Ended up with a big bald patch. She was taken to the doctor, the same one who would soon casually addict our mother to Valium. *Ah yes*, he said wisely, *alopecia*. Mum put him right. He prescribed something calming - his answer to all female distress - and hat wearing. I gently steered her fingers away whenever she tried to get through the woolly cap and in a few weeks the compulsion faded away.

My sister was clever, sociable, funny. Yes, that's the past tense.

I moved away to university when she was only nine, feeling terrible about leaving her in such an unhappy household. Mum was long past any conversation by then and the family was already deep in disaster territory. But I still believed dad was dependable and anyone could see how much he loved my little sister, and she him.

I can't sum up a life in a few hundred words. How could I choose what to include and what to leave out? Her story could be told a thousand ways. It's hers to tell but she's no longer here to tell it. So it falls to me and I know I am inadequate to the task. I can only tell the story of us, and I can only tell it from my side.

We were sisters. So things got complicated. I loved her but I also found her difficult; I know she felt the same about me. She struggled to get out from under the label of *little sister*, to be taken seriously as an adult; I was slow to relinquish the authority of *big sister*. Once she had looked up to me, copied me, adopting my interests and attitudes. Then, inevitably, I disappointed her by proving myself fallible, inconsistent, selfish.

We were full of contradictions. I was too *political* for her tastes, she was too *spiritual* for mine. Neither descriptor a compliment. I was the one who fancied myself a rebel against consumerism, yet studied my way into professional positions that paid half-decent money; she was the one who decorated her home with crystals and angels yet got sucked into crazy fortune-promising pyramid schemes. The anti-capitalist member of the salitariat versus the spiritual fortune hunter whose impossible dream was to retire to the beach at thirty. We didn't make a lot of sense.

Her last few years were hard but we had some good times all the same. Sitting outside her back door smoking - relaxed and chatting about whatever, nothing in particular. Her daughters, her friends, her weird next door neighbour, the adventures of her peripatetic cat. Going to the pictures together, forgettable but fun science fiction, thrillers. Easy company, we'd earned it.

I have put a photo up in my writing room, the one her younger daughter gave me of me and her in Hackney from way back, a photo taken by our dad. We're outdoors, looking happy. I'm the taller one, grinning, denim-jacketed, leaning casually on her shoulder while she stands four-square, rooted, comfortable, in her bright pink soft summer blazer. I have put a poem next to it and I look at the picture and read the poem and give it a few seconds and it feels like a positive little ritual of acceptance and gladness of having known her. I didn't plan it that way, it just seems to have happened.

Because it's so hard to remember the good times. It's a special problem with people who kill themselves. Grief and anger makes it hard to access the good stuff, to remember the love. There is so much pain to get through first. Pain that results directly from what they did, their terrible gift. From the unbearable choice they made. That, ending all their dreams, they were forced to make.

The Square on the Hypotenuse

Black objects absorb heat better than white ones. The sun is approximately 93 million miles away. The square on the hypotenuse equals the sum of the squares on the other two sides. But only in a right angled triangle. Don't rely on that rule if you find yourself in an isosceles triangle or, worse, a circle. Then you'd never get out. Or know if your car would make it assuming the petrol tank is leaking at 25 millilitres per second, your maximum speed is 20 mph and the nearest garage is closed.

My brother is three years younger than me. I haven't seen him since my mother's funeral fifteen years ago. My sister was nine years younger than me. She took her own life nine years ago. Do the arithmetic. Who didn't go to whose funeral? Do you have enough information?

Elephants never forget. Goldfish forget everything every ten seconds. That's what I've been told anyway. Which would you rather? Bee or a wasp? Sorry that's my father sneaking in again, terrible man for his puns. My father died seventeen years ago. He had a strong heart so it took him a very long time to forget everything. When he forgot how to swallow we let him go. My brother came to his funeral. So did my sister. My mother didn't. But she was unwell and the funeral was far away. My parents got divorced a very long time ago. Is any of this of any interest? Discuss.

The universe started with a big bang. Or was it just one in an infinite series of big bangs? In which case what does starting mean? If the tortoise gets a head start, who wins, the tortoise or the hare? A little knowledge is a dangerous thing. But curiosity killed the cat. And faith can move mountains. Though there appears to be no peer-reviewed, authoritatively-verified evidence that it ever has.

Get the facts. That was my father's mantra. I can still hear him say it, head doggedly down, using his deepest register and great emphasis. Let's – get – the – facts! He was a physical scientist. Could you guess? He also did a yogic headstand every morning, was a jazz saxophonist and wasn't averse to getting stoned from time to time. Bet you didn't guess that, did you. You didn't have enough information.

CRY BABY

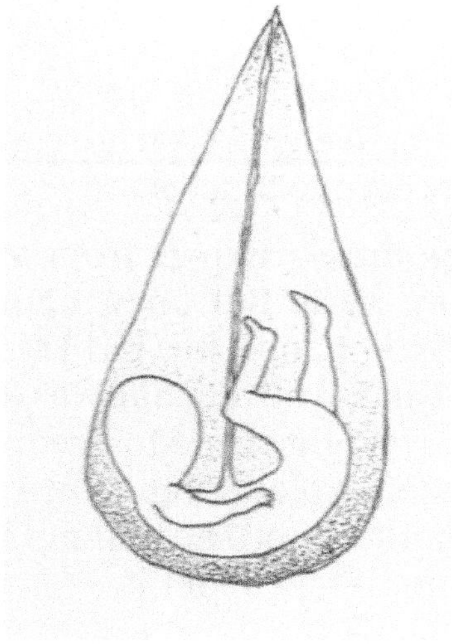

Boys, Men, Sex: A Brief Overview of the Main Events

Kiss Catch (9) Running away from the boys, shrieking, trying to ensure you are caught by the right one, the one everyone fancies.

First Orgasm (?) Expert from an early age. No idea what they were. But knew enough not to talk about them. Except once, to a girl I somehow thought would understand. And did. She was dismissive of my hypothesis they might relate to needing the toilet but offered no other explanation. When I tried to raise the subject another time she told me she'd given it up and didn't want to talk about it.

First Kiss (12) In a small carpark. Three years older than me, separated by an unbridgeable gulf of sophistication (his). Chucked me after about a month. Strongest memory - sitting beside the river disagreeing over whether you'd be electrocuted if you swung across the water on the power lines. He was right as I later found out. You wouldn't.

First Time (almost 14) Also three years older. Mechanic. Saw him every week at swimming club. Found the courage to ask him out to a dance; he agreed so long as it was understood he wouldn't actually dance. Three months later, after much enthusiastic messing about, he asked if I'd go all the way. I said I'd have to think about it. Decided I loved him; therefore told him next day it was OK. And it was. After his family moved away we wrote, I visited once. (Long distance calls were expensive.) Later he crashed his motorbike and married his then girlfriend. I reckoned it'd been her bedside manner. Though I'd always known I wouldn't marry him.

First Longer Term Relationship (16 - 20) By now I was worldly wise. If a better understanding of electricity counts. And the fact that I had lost count of bedpost notches around fifty. Very keen to plunge into psychedelics and reject the trappings of conventionality. Spotted and groomed by the local expert in the field. Guitarist, small scale cannabis dealer, yada yada. Twelve years older than me. Ego the size of a mountain. First year a lot of fun. Subsequent years very much downhill. One event in particular caused me to burn with shame for decades. He's dead now.

Interval (21 - 29) Got away to London, got into politics, squatting, feminism. Came out. Cried when a woman gave me back my body.

Second Long Term Relationship (29 - 40) Two greatest loves of my life - aforementioned woman and this man. Never saw him lose his temper or ability to play the blues, however drunk. Quietly left the room whenever I cried, which was seldom. Cultivated a suave exterior; fedoras and sharp suits. Fabulous cheekbones. Many good years followed by communication collapse and earth-shattering betrayal. (He's also dead.)

Third Long Term Relationship (42 - 52) Trotskyist. Activist. Jazz fiend. Never lived together. Weekends, holidays. Think we just faded away in the end. Though he survives and we remain friends. All you need to know.

One more attempt, then that seems to be that. Suppose it's theoretically possible somebody might wake me up again but hard to imagine. Would never have believed sex could come to mean so little to me. But then life is full of surprises.

Missing Link

There's a missing link here. How did I get from the earnest thirteen year old who needed to check in with herself that she 'loved' her boyfriend before she could have sex with him to the sixteen year old who lost count of her sexual partners?

I don't think it's a coincidence that it was during this time that young girl found out, first, her mum was an alcoholic, and second, she wasn't going to stop drinking, and third, her dad was useless in this context.

But that doesn't answer the question. It merely provides the backdrop.

What was her promiscuity like? What was it about? Who was she?

Her first experience of sex had been good. Affectionate, consensual, no great power imbalance, fun. There was at least one subsequent boyfriend that she didn't have sex with, so there must have been a period when she was still applying the 'love' rules.

But soon that changed.

There was a boyfriend she had sex with who she definitely never imagined she loved.

I also remember her pursuing a young man relentlessly who couldn't have made it clearer (kindly) that he didn't want to go to bed with her. She couldn't understand his reluctance but more importantly she didn't care. So she badgered him till he did the job.

What did she want? She had no delusions about becoming his girlfriend; it was clear that wasn't going to happen. I remember she got up early the next morning and walked home. How was she feeling? Pleased she'd achieved her objective. Pleased she could add him to the lengthening list of people she had had sex with. Even though she knew perfectly well he hadn't really wanted to. I don't remember her having any 'nasty' feelings about him. She wasn't gloating, She was mildly grateful. She didn't pursue him any further. She had got what she thought she wanted.

I remember her lying in bed counting her sexual partners. I remember her being able to get to about fifty. Who were they? I remember her trying this exercise later and not being able to get even half way. I'd struggle now to remember more than five.

She had found out her mum didn't love her. She was fifteen.

But it wasn't love she was looking for, was it? It doesn't sound like that to me. Though it's possible I just can't bear to admit it. To me, it feels more like a desire for control. She couldn't control her home situation but she could get guys to have sex with her.

Why did she choose sex as one of her methods to exercise control? (Academic dominance being the other.) As a young woman in a tiny northern town in the early 1970s did she see sex as one of the few sources of power available to her? One of the few available indicators of success? Could she really have failed to notice the rules were different for girls?

Looking back now, her behaviour might seem desperate, pathetic. She was missing something. She was trying to fill herself up with something. She was refusing to be rejected. Her mum had rejected her but nobody else was going to be allowed to? She was seeking connection on the most basic crude level?

Or did she imagine that she was beating the boys at their own game, like she already was in maths and science? God knows it was an easy game to pick. It's not hard to get lads to have sex with you when you're a teenager. In any case, having disassociated sex from love, and even desire, she was ready for her First Longer Term Relationship.

A Man in Possession of a Truth

First Longer Term Relationship was intense. He was in possession of some kind of truth, a truth he was never able to communicate to me. A truth I tacitly subscribed to as a condition of our relationship. It was something to do with a higher consciousness achieved through smoking a lot of cannabis and playing a guitar and being him. Mandalas may have come into it.

He felt greatly superior to anyone not in possession of this truth. But he could also be smooth, a snake charmer. Men, particularly, seemed to take him at face value, unaware of the deep contempt in which he held them.

Early on, while I was still living in my parents' house, we came to blows. He said something that placed me firmly below any acceptable level of consciousness. Something like I had no soul, I only operated on the material plane. I don't remember exactly. But I fully understood the depth of insult intended.

As he started walking away downstairs, I leaned over the bannister and took a swipe at his head. He turned, charged back up and threw himself at me. We rolled about on the landing, trying to land punches. The noise alerted my father who came running up and pulled us apart. This was not the way differences of opinion were settled in my family.

My brother told me later that FLTR had looked green as my father walked him down the stairs.

You must have got him in the balls.

A rare moment of fraternal admiration. My brother never fell for FLTR's charm. Though, aware of his own self-interest, he generally adopted a suitably deferential attitude.

Physical violence was rare; FLTR much preferred emotional abuse. Except for two or three times, during sex, when he got angry and started strangling me. It was always brief, I never came anywhere near passing out, but the helpless struggle for breath was frightening. He never apologised; none of those tearful protestations of remorse and reform I've read about. Not at all. I think he assumed I'd deserved it and it was up to me to do better next time. I don't think I bought that - I don't think I ever thought it was my fault. But why I tolerated it and came back for more is a much harder question.

I've worked out an answer that makes sense to me, looking back down forty years. But I'd love to know what that girl would have said at the time. Would it have been different?

Status

So what first attracted you to...

Are you kidding? First Longer Term Relationship was the lead guitarist in the best band in town. He was a constant supply of cannabis. He was twelve years older than me. Being his girlfriend conferred small town status to dream of.

Though I certainly wouldn't have admitted that at the time. Once, a girl at school asked me if I was still going out with him. When I confirmed it she said, *Oh, you are so lucky!* I felt embarrassed - for her.

Did I fancy him? Irrelevant. I was prepared to get used to having sex with him. And his bald head. I only discovered years later that some people thought getting off with a schoolie while aged 28 was a great achievement for him. That idea had never occurred to me.

A desire for status drove much of my teenage behaviour. I was hugely competitive, revised manically for exams and was only satisfied by coming first in every subject I considered important i.e. anything taught for more than an hour each week. At the same time I worked hard at being a classroom rebel. It no longer seems funny or clever to me to clip clothes pegs to the back of our vulnerable Maths teacher's shabby suit jacket. Or to enter his room concealing a burning joss stick behind my back. Or to point out every tiny mistake he made in his blackboard calculations.

In my final year I was threatened with suspension for skiving off triple Chemistry on Tuesday afternoons, time I preferred to spend smoking with FLTR. I refused to reform, instead speculating on how I might cope academically if I was suspended. When the deputy head pointed out the school couldn't treat me differently from everyone else I said, politely, that was their problem, not mine. I was counting on them not wanting to threaten the results of one of their star pupils. I was right, heard no more about it and, after the usual ferocious revision, aced all my exams. I saw this as a great victory for my Simultaneously Top Of The Class And The Naughtiest Girl In The School strategy and reflected smugly on it for years. But soon this pursuit of status became toxic.

I got into Imperial College where I found myself spending a good deal of time in the silent library, head down, laboriously following the logic from one tortuous equation to the next. Although I did well in my first year, I finally had to face the fact that I would never be top of the class. I could never eat, breathe and talk only of Maths like the top half dozen boys did. I tried to convince myself that being in the top ten of over a hundred was a worthwhile goal but failed. In the second year my visits to the library tailed off and then stopped altogether.

Much more seriously, a year later, when forced to return home, discharged from the psych ward into my father's care, the shame I felt was life-threatening. Now I'd become a poster girl for pride coming before a fall.

A Moroccan Adventure

It was the summer before I went to university. I was seventeen. First Longer Term Relationship and I hitched to Morocco in search of a hash farm in the mountains of Ketama. And found one. Where we were treated as honoured guests despite making it clear we had no money to speak of. Alarm bells should have been ringing.

On the second night, sleeping on cushions round the sitting room, I was woken by a kiss in the pitch dark. I responded for a moment, until my hands found a full head of hair. Appalled, I pushed the kisser away, hissing *No*, frightened of waking my hot-tempered travelling companion. Second mistake. I should have shouted. Seventeen.

Next day all carried on as normal. Unlimited excellent hash, friendliness all round. We went swimming in a mountain pool though FLTR didn't get in. The Moroccan lads urged me to take off my t-shirt. I didn't. Lots of laughing, no problem, all good fun. No other women there of course. The Moroccan women worked ceaselessly, fetching wood and water, baking bread, cooking over open fires, looking after the kids, harvesting and drying the cannabis. Dressed in long layers of charity shop cast offs, rubber boots. The men ran the business, sat around all day smoking kief and being waited on, drove flash cars. Lads wore branded Western casuals, older men dressed traditionally.

Several days later I found myself alone in a car with the kisser, the second son of the family we were staying with. I had no concerns, we were friends now after all. Then he stopped the car. Started begging me to have sex with him. I was shocked. I refused. He persisted. I got out of the car and started walking the deserted mountain road. I had no idea where I was and no hope of getting safely back to the farm. He pulled up beside me, apologising profusely. I got back in. He resumed driving. Rinse and repeat. The third or fourth time I'd had enough. It was obvious I was bluffing. By now he was in tears as he pleaded. His English was excellent. I felt sick.

We got in the back. It didn't take long. Afterwards he drove us back to the farm. I was silent, thinking. He put his hand on my leg and said sorry. That was the worst moment.

It was imperative FLTR didn't find out. I knew he'd go crazy. Over the next day or two the atmosphere changed. The kisser's mother was furious, shouting at him every time she saw him. She continued being friendly and kind to me, without us having any common language.

Then I received an invitation to visit the hajji. Just me. She was an elderly woman, the only one in the village who had made the pilgrimage to Mecca. The kisser spoke to me in a very serious tone, emphasising this was a huge honour. Grimly, I told him I understood.

I behaved impeccably. We nodded and smiled wordlessly at each other. We shared food from the usual communal plate, just the two of us. The women even made it easy for me to eat an appropriately tiny amount by serving the only meal I hated, offal.

Next day things moved fast. It was made clear to my bemused companion that we must leave immediately. We were driven to the bus station in Ketama. The kisser and his friends followed at a distance in his car. I was very frightened, FLTR was oblivious. We got away safely. But it wasn't the end of the matter.

A Moroccan Adventure Part 2

I dropped out of university in my second year. I was nineteen and bitterly disappointed by the lack of radical hedonism that, incredibly, I'd imagined I'd find at Imperial College. I'd also discovered I only enjoyed Pure Maths; all Applied Maths was boring as fuck. And compulsory. I didn't like doing things I didn't like. And I'd had a better offer.

First Longer Term Relationship had resurfaced and sold me on the idea of a commune in Aberdeenshire. Dope, freedom, fresh air, another opportunity to stick it to the man. I packed my bags.

Strangely enough, unlimited hash and very little to do suited neither of us well. He became positively Messianic, preaching incessantly to the gang of six he'd managed to accumulate, impressing upon us his ability to transport us wherever he chose by the power of his guitar playing. *Sure.* He also asserted that he could read my mind - a claim that was easily disproved by lying under him smiling, projecting *I hate you* as hard as I could.

Perhaps unsurprisingly, he became obsessed with the idea there was something I was hiding from him. He bullied me mercilessly, demanding access to every corner of my mind, every private thought. Eventually, in desperation, I offered up the information that I'd 'had sex' with the kisser in Morocco. (I was yet to understand it was rape.)

He was enraged. I had trashed his authority, his masculinity, his status. I had made him look a fool. From then on I was dirt beneath his boots. Day by day, night by night, eyes burning with hate, he destroyed me with his words and his body. In that stifling dusty room, in the blistering summer of '76, in front of everyone. There was no defence, nobody came to my aid; his narrative had long been the only one possible. Within a few weeks I was admitted to the psych ward of an Aberdeen hospital, out of my mind, convinced tanks were appearing over the hill.

That was the end of me and him. But it still wasn't the end of the matter.

When 'Having Sex' Is Being Raped

How did I come to realise this? And why was it so hard?

The starting point was, surely, in the late 1970s after I had got away from FLTR. Getting involved with the women's liberation movement in London, sharing experiences with other women, developing an understanding of how male supremacy works and how it had got so deep into my head. How I'd learned to scorn myself, hate myself. That cruel internal voice tormenting me with my inadequacies, my general disgustingness, my sticky femaleness.

That voice is so much quieter now. I remember, in my twenties, being stunned when, berating myself in an NHS counselling session for some folly or other, I was asked by my counsellor, *How would you feel if it was your best friend who had done that?*

It stopped me in my tracks. I took a moment to imagine it. And was amazed when a completely different feeling surged upwards through my body. A rising tide of kindness, of empathy, of affection, *Oh you silly sausage,* a tide of love.

Why can't you be your own best friend? Why indeed?

I know now this is Counselling 101. I've seen it in a load of self-help texts (not that I am a fan of these) but it was new to me then. But this wasn't about acquiring some novel intellectual understanding. It was the physical response of my body that was so enlightening. The way warmth rose up me like the softest bath towel absorbing all the tension, wiping away the hurt, blotting out the vicious words. From then on, whenever the little voice started up, I would imagine it was my best friend and lover who was guilty of whatever sin was being enumerated. Then I would pay attention to my physical sensations.

It was very significant for me that this epiphany was originating from my body. It was my body doing something amazing. I'd long considered my body little more than an unreliable, unsatisfactory appendage dangling from where the real action was, in my head, where I lived. (The only thing my body seemed to be good at was pleasing men.) I was starting to develop a new relationship with my body. I was starting to understand that my body was part of me. That I was my body. That insults to my body were insults to me.

I had to begin to stop hating myself before I could feel any entitlement to not being treated like shit. Before I could even realise that I was being treated like shit. Obvious really.

Working at the Bank

I have a broad grin and a flash of full, friendly, eye contact for everyone; you've taken the paper I'm holding out before you know it. It'd feel rude not to. And the paper's OK, it's just some kind of entertainment guide, there's no scam involved. It's harmless and there are litter bins everywhere you can dump it in anyway.

Winter 1978. Exit Bank tube early on a Friday morning and there I am. Not always at the same exit. So you can't plan to avoid me. It used to take the supervisor a while to find me. But they soon appreciate me for the rare pearl I am, someone who is actually giving the job her all. No need to check. Much cheaper to just give me the Employee of the Week bullshit from time to time; makes me laugh that they'd think I care. I don't need anything from them, except a few quid. They must think I'm either very stupid or some kind of nutcase. Anyway it's exactly the sort of stupidity or nuttiness they need so it seems everyone's happy.

And people don't feel bad seeing me handing out free newspapers in the freezing London dawn as they hurry past in their suits. This is my real gift, the sharpest tool in my kit. There is no way you can feel guilty about me. I'm enjoying myself and you can see it. If you only knew, I feel sorry for you, chained to your hamster wheel, running your rodent race. I'm blessed, blissed out, no earphones needed, I've got Hendrix murmuring in my ear, *stoned, immaculate.* You'll never hear him.

Second Long Term Relationship

Become friends. It feels safe - you're both spoken for and you follow the rules. Laughing and horsing about on three a.m. walks across town back to your respective homes from FLTR's mother's place. Where the band hang out thanks to her relaxed attitude to the consumption of cannabis.

Enjoy group activities together. West Coast American psychedelic rock. Walking by the shore in the night, getting stoned in long lazy afternoons skiving off school, just your crew. LSD - till you have a bad one. Music. Always music.

Have one glorious weekend in bed. Other halves both away. No big romance, just two good mates finding out how to drive each other crazy.

Get found out. FLTR's attitude to free love exposed - strictly for him, not you. Status quo resumes, bumpily.

Fall into bed together at longish intervals over the next few years. No expectations, no strings; he usually has someone else on the go, conveniently long distance. You're between partners. The sex is great. And you enjoy each other's company. Neither of you are doing romance. You feel no guilt. His dishonesty - if any - is his business.

Fall into bed again but this time neither of you is attached. Business as usual initially. But now there's no need for longish intervals so you start seeing each other more often. Why not? You're both having a lovely time. You reassure each other - still no strings. Go through the charade of asking the other every time if it's OK to stay over. You know it's a turning point the day you reply that you'd be disappointed if he didn't.

Continue for a couple of years.

Move in together. Your place. Split rent, split bills, own bedrooms, sleep together at the weekends. Sex remains great. He looks after himself, you never iron a shirt. You look after yourself too. Sometimes you eat together, he cooks more often. Own lives, both working, studying, he gets another band together, starts gigging. They're good but you get increasingly bored of their set.

Officialise the monogamy that's been happening anyway. Or at least agree to tell the other if anything else should occur. It doesn't.

Independence paired with passionate connection; having your cake and eating it. Life is good.

Slip into romance almost without noticing. Or at least you do. You're not sure whether he does; he's a firm adherent to the need-to-know principle. And there's so much you don't need to know. He honours the agreement though - confesses to a meaningless drunken fumble, too pissed to be consummated. You accept comforting hugs. You're glad he told you but decline the accompanying funny stories he offers.

Start thinking about having a baby. That's you, not him. Agree to put the idea on hold for a couple of years. Continue working, studying. The idea grows but you are conflicted. You don't talk about it. You're worried that if you push it, it'll split you up. And you're not sure which you want more. You're conflicted. Worth saying twice.

Stop using contraception. He starts.

Begin lying to yourself. Lazy lies that wouldn't stand up to scrutiny. So you don't scrutinise them.

Finally speak. He denies all knowledge of anything being on hold. Drawls *Having children is a pastime for one's declining years*. You note - scream, shout - that it wouldn't be with you in that case. Biology being what it is. To which he has no answer.

The end

It Says Nothing

She says I love you.

He says nothing.

It says nothing to him, what she says. It says nothing - no that's not quite true. It says I want you to say you love me. It says I want to trap you, I want you to commit to me in a way that you will regret and will cause you suffering at some unspecified future date. It says that he would be wise to keep his mouth shut at this point.

She says nothing. It says nothing to her that he says nothing - no that's not quite true. It says that she is a strong independent woman. It says that she doesn't need to hear him say he loves her. It says that she is a mistress of self-deception.

She says she loves him again, several days later. She says it and then she immediately turns away on some inconsequential errand. She says it like this to show him, to show him how complete she is in herself, how much she doesn't need to hear him say it.

She says it whenever she feels like it, which is quite often; she is scrupulous never to say it with any expectation that he will reply in kind.

He says it twice in the ten years they are together. He says it once at the moment of orgasm; she discounts this because their sex life is good so his utterance can reasonably be regarded as an involuntary ejaculation.

It says something that she can never remember what the other occasion was.

It says something that she can never work out what it is that it says.

How to Make a Baby

1. Decide you want one.

    Don't make your mind up aged twelve, before you realise that lives of quiet desperation are the norm, that you'd rather die than do anything your parents have done.

2. Don't listen to your mother when she tells you, around the same time, not to have children, that children ruin your life.

    Up until then you thought your mother loved you, didn't you? Though to be fair she did have three of us. So it might not have been you.

3. Don't make it your publicly stated life goal to kill yourself when you reach thirty; see lives of quiet desperation above.

    That just doesn't leave enough time to have a baby properly unless you're one of those stupid irresponsible girls. Which you are not. Quite the opposite, your mother has told you from an early age that you are unusually intelligent. Your mother has told you a few things.

4. Don't fall in love with a man who doesn't want to make a baby.

Who already made one and it didn't work out well. Shotgun wedding, the baby lived for a day, and the mother went off with the guy next door.

5. Don't lie to yourself about your relationship with the man.

For example, don't tell yourself that eventually he will feel like he owes you a baby. That is ridiculous. Of course he won't. You know him better than that. Though you couldn't have been expected to know that he would swear black is white the subject had never been discussed when you clearly remember agreeing a two-year moratorium while you studied for a postgraduate degree on your day off.

6. Don't get diagnosed with a Serious Mental Illness.

Because the man now feels somewhat cheated. He is sure you told him you came with a clean bill of health. And obviously he's not going to make a baby with someone who has a Serious Mental Illness. Who do you think he is?

7. Be born a few years later so you can benefit from advances in medical technology.

8. Don't have a hysterectomy when you are forty-two years old.

Leaving The Cabbage Patch

Cabbages are so endearing. Who can resist that little green face peering up from its mob cap of leaves? The poignancy of its dependence. The charm of its fear. Because they do know, they do know that being ripped from the earth is not the prelude to anything good.

Freezing night, impossibly paired with glaring light. Then wrapped in plastic, isolated from air and water, a half-life requiring a gritty determination to survive, a level of determination never needed before, never needed while the sun shone and the rain fell and the attention of the occasional slug was all that must be endured.

Time passes. She enters the supermarket, examines the display. Those little cabbages, some coy, half hidden, some bold, looking right back at her. What temperament of cabbage will complement her mood? How much does she want one? She's bored today, doesn't want to engage, picks almost at random.

Back home, unpacking. The cabbage, liberated from polythene shroud, chills in the fridge. It's dark and there is moisture in the air and some quiet company. The cabbage relaxes a little. Perhaps food will come. The cabbage is a survivor, a pragmatist. It's seen others succumb to sun and slug; it understands the value of patience, of persistence.

Dawn bursts in. Night falls, moments later. The cabbage is unsettled but the others seem unruffled so, again, it calms. Days of incredible shortness flash past. Eventually the cabbage is chosen again, lifted, set on a wooden slab. The day is already longer.

It looks up at the woman standing in front of it. Its little green face is so cute, its leaves so artfully arranged; she picked a good one despite her lack of care. Reaching round that forever empty child-shaped ache, she smiles and picks up the knife.

A Moroccan Adventure Part 3 or Revenge At The Lighthouse

Flash forward. I'm 52, visiting the old home town where my step brothers and I have organised a celebration of my dad's life. It's a widely advertised open-to-all bash as my dad would have wanted and First Longer Term Relationship's band is providing the music. Long story. My dad was also a musician and had enjoyed playing with him. In the distant past I'd asked him to sever all ties but, as I couldn't possibly reveal why - to my dad, c'mon, and you haven't heard the half of it either - he had declined to do so. I spent a lot of time outside the hall that night, standing with friends and coping (well) with my ancient notoriety. But lots of people came up and shared fond stories of my dad and it was a really good night.

I spoke briefly with FLTR and arranged to visit him the following day to buy a sizable chunk of hash. One of his nephews drove me out to the remote lighthouse cottage he had bought many years ago when the lighthouse became fully automated. I was on excellent form. Just hyper enough to be confident, articulate, aware of my environment, able to read the room. Feeling on top of my game.

The inevitable bong was produced. We smoked, chatted, reminisced over some of our more amusing memories. A couple of other people were there. He brought up what he thought would be an excruciatingly embarrassing incident. It wasn't. Hadn't been for years. Then he brought up the kisser. I looked him straight in the eye.

M raped me.

Silence.

M raped me in the back of his car. Every word enunciated.

He could see I was telling the truth.

I'd have killed him! Bombastically, the idiot.

Yeah, and then they'd have killed you.

I spoke with contempt.

And then, there I'd be, sitting there surrounded by dead men. I'd probably never have got out. I'd probably still be there.

Silence.

I. Was. Saving. Your. Life...

Every word a sentence. A life sentence. Every word a stab to his guts. He'd vilified me for years over this.

... And I don't regret it. My dad got a lot out of playing with you.

The room sat silent, eyes down.

Him. *I wondered why that woman was running after the car shouting 'Thank you'.*

I hadn't noticed that. It was good to know.

Why didn't you tell me? You said you'd had sex with him.

I was confused. I felt guilty. I was too young to understand.

Quietly, *No wonder you ended up in hospital.*

* * *

But the crowning glory came right at the end as I was leaving, after all the flowery apologies. To which I had given no more than the slightest nod of acknowledgement.

They all knew the bones of my Second Long Term Relationship and why it had collapsed. It was a very small town and, remember, SLTR had been the other guitarist in the band, back in my teenage days.

I was halfway out the door, hash in pocket, feeling good.

He muttered, *I'd have given you a kiddie. With your intelligence and my...* Somehow the end of the sentence eluded him.

FLTR - the man who'd groomed me, abused me, shamed me, driven me insane.

I caught the nephew's eye and we fell out the door, collapsing into hysterical laughter. Bent double, gasping and shrieking, totally out of control. After everything that had just been revealed. It was too much. It was glorious. And we were wrecked.

When I eventually recovered I stood up tall and raised my voice to the heavens. A cry of great pain. A cry of triumph and fury.

I didnae want yer kiddie! I wanted S's kiddie!

I turned to my driver and told him I would be back in a minute, was just going to take a quick look out at the end of the headland. It was night and the haar had rolled in, blanketing everything in a smoky darkness. I took a few deep breaths of the cool salty air. This had been a momentous reckoning and I wanted to savour it to the full.

When I returned FLTR was standing in his doorway, head down, a pitch-perfect portrayal of humiliation. I spoke to my driver, the nephew.

You were right. There's nothing to see.

I reached out and raised FLTR's chin with my crooked forefinger. Like you'd do to a child.

Then we left.

I never saw him again.

Starting Again Somewhere Else

Babies have a hundred more bones than adults do. This makes them crunchier. You can chew them up and spit them out more easily. Though, because the bones are smaller and thinner, you may find they get stuck between your teeth. I recommend flossing.

Alternatively you can extract them and create a delicate lattice work, like spun sugar, much more complex and beautiful than anything you could make with those great lumpen adult femurs and whatnot. This makes a lovely wall hanging for a nursery.

A spinster aunt of my acquaintance arranged her set so meticulously, integrating them with slivers of coal and stringing them with cobwebs, that she was able to play the jolliest tunes her visitors had ever heard. Her singalongs were legendary; invitations bartered for gold.

Another created an elegant basket which she placed in the hall near her front door. Dolorous black umbrellas wept there for decades on her behalf, freeing her for a life of fragrant indulgence.

A friend built a wildly irregular picket fence with hers to fend off the crowds of emperor penguins who had gathered to stare judgmentally through her windows. This brought some relief though the lack of an integrated garage meant she still had to run a daily gauntlet to her car.

One woman I know used them to spell out scatological imperatives which she projected onto the exterior walls of her house, finally ridding herself of sympathisers and scolds alike. Her landlady took photos and between them they won a prestigious art prize.

Mine have always shattered like breadcrumbs, laying a gleaming trail behind me however deep in the forest I wander. Forever leading me back. One day I'll walk away from them and start again somewhere else.

AT THE MOUNTAINS OF MADNESS

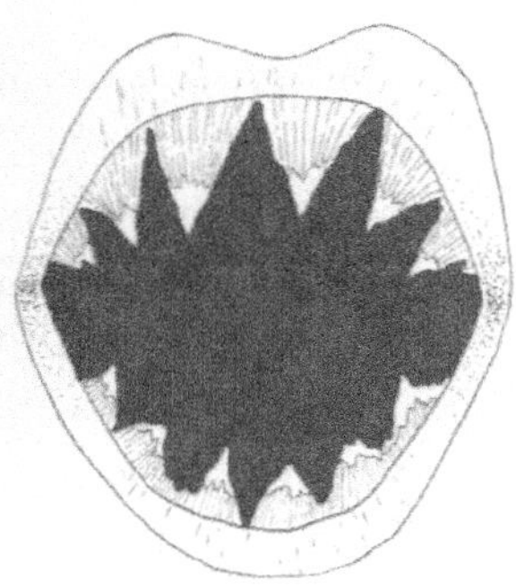

Driving to the End of the World

When I was 16 my dad took me out in our old grey Ford Consul. Rural roads, little traffic, not much to go wrong. Until I saw my current crush and started frantically waving. *Me, driving a car, cool eh?* My dad went bonkers. I didn't get it. He had weird priorities. A bit later, when I was driving straight towards a large plastic bag, he told me to avoid it. *You can't be sure it's empty.* This time I understood. Imperfect information, got it.

I couldn't afford driving lessons till my mid-twenties. By then, thanks to the 1977 GLC squatting amnesty, me and a couple of other women shared a hard-to-let Hackney Council flat. Early one evening a knock on the door revealed my driving instructor. Shit! I had forgotten all about it, so was much more stoned than I would have been otherwise; I was stoned all the time in those days and, let's be fair, for a long time afterwards. There seemed no option but to follow the gangly Jamaican downstairs and get in the driving seat. He did get a bit grumpy when I kept turning the windscreen wipers on before turning corners but it wasn't our usual car so I had some excuse.

After I passed my test I bought an ancient minivan and racked up three months of London driving before the brakes failed. Fixing them was way beyond my means; I liked driving but resigned myself to doing without it.

Then a job came up where I worked – Bookbus Driver. With incredible chutzpah I applied. Women bus drivers were a rarity in 1984 and Hackney was Red Labour – the first London borough to include lesbians and gays in their Equal Opportunities Policy. A woman driving their big yellow bus would be good visuals. They already knew I was a book addict – on lunch breaks from my clerical job I headed down the old town hall stairs buried deep in a book. And now I was going to learn to drive an ancient Routemaster, a full size double-decker with no power steering and a crash gearbox.

Which I did. Eventually. Beginning by stalling it eight or nine times from the sheer terror of feeling this unfathomably enormous monster inch backwards. Yes, my instructor made me start in reverse; buses have no rear view mirror. We were on an East London airfield but that didn't help. The first time he left me alone to drive a few hundred yards, turn the bus round, and drive it back, I managed to reverse into a shed. Probably the only shed for miles.

That walk of shame... *The back window's busted, a padlock went through it.*

But the guys – yep, they were all guys – were great and everyone stuck with me till I made it. My first instructor was a tiny elf, used a wooden box in the cab, told me he was an ex ballet dancer though you couldn't believe a word any of them said. When signing me off, the head guy told my manager I'd crashed – then hurriedly reassured him – *No, no, Sarah gave us a lovely ride.* Cue more splutterings on the other end of the line.

But my hairiest driving adventure came later. Bursting with energy, overwhelmed with the urge to go and see my best friend up north, oblivious to any notion that this might be a bad idea, I set off in the middle of the night.

As I tore up the deserted motorway my hypomania increased. I became sure the world was ending, the only uncertainty was whether it already had. A lot of the time there seemed no sign of life. Then headlights would appear on the other side of the central reservation and I'd think *OK, not yet then.* I didn't feel anything much, none of it was personal, it was all like a film somehow.

Approaching Manchester I started to realise things were not quite making sense and decided to detour to my sister in Warrington. Her turn to pick up the pieces.

Tower of Babel

In 1994 some Eastern European psychiatric hospitals used bed cages. Maybe they still do, I don't know. But I know they did in 1994 because that was when I found myself in one. Naked. Without access to water or a toilet. Unable to leave the bed. Unable to stand up.

The bed was surrounded by other women. With clothes on. There was quite a bit of excited talking in a language I didn't understand and some laughing. I didn't care that I was naked. I didn't mind the laughing, it seemed fair enough. I was in a great mood, laughing along, hypomanic not psychotic. I knew what sort of place I was in and I understood what was happening.

The women were kind. I was thirsty, miming my need for water. One of them mimed back - nowhere to pee, so no water. I hammed up my desperation, my pitiful pleading, to more laughter. I've always liked making people laugh. After a while the same woman let me drink a little water - *malo, malo* - through a straw between the bars.

I was left in the bed cage all night. Unable to sleep, I sang Mercedes Benz at volume for a long time. I know all the words. I could hear the staff, at some distance, talking and laughing. I heard one say *Janis Joplin* and this pleased me. I've worked hard on my Janis Joplin impersonation.

This was a work trip gone wrong. As a last-minute replacement, I was helping a colleague deliver a training course. There to fetch and carry and lead a single session, on a topic I had been unable to get any kind of briefing about, which made me very anxious. My session was a disaster of course. But that wasn't the problem.

The problem was the colleague. She spoke to her audience in a jolly, childish manner, trying to encourage their participation by asking absurdly easy questions. When, entirely reasonably, they refused to humiliate themselves by answering, she just dumbed the question down a little further. It was excruciating. These were adults, operating fluently in their second or third language, and she was addressing them as if they were idiots. I became increasingly distressed.

Her eyes became frightening. Black holes in the front of her head; nothing behind them. They made no connection, they led only to a dark empty skull. Her smiling, mindless countenance never changed. I felt terribly sorry for her. After one session I sat with one of the course participants, both of us in tears, desperately trying to reassure ourselves that actually she liked being like that.

But when the men in white coats arrived at our hotel it was me they'd come to take away, unmoved by my uncollegial cries of, *It's her! She's the mad one.*

I was let out of the bed cage the next day and spent a few more days in hospital before my sister - no stranger to my incarcerations and quite excited by her exotic foreign trip - arrived to fly home with me. A kind Jewish doctor had let me spend most of the time writing in his room away from the bustle of a ward where no-one spoke my language.

Later, when I tried to return to work, it turned out my employers didn't speak my language either.

High School Reunion

What are you doing here? Incredulous, heavy emphasis on the third word. Delivered, as I enter the foyer, by a guy I recognise, always a maverick but one of the most irritating. Weirdly tolerated by many, not so much by me. It's a good question though. What the hell am I doing here, in this crowd of forty-year-old ex-pupils? I only ever hung out with two or three girl friends at school and when they left the year before me (Scottish versus English universities, avoid boring digression) I was a loner, doing all my socialising elsewhere. Today I've arrived thin skinned, far out of any comfort zone. Now I draw that old familiar flak jacket round me and snarl at him *I went to this fucking school too*. Good start. Very Janis Joplin. Though without the stellar career or the feathers.

People ask me to park round the corner. This is a girl I hung out with a bit, not one of my inner circle. She's now a community psychiatric nurse, married with one son, still living and working in the town. Takes me a moment to get it. So I tell her I'm bipolar. I refuse to be part of this shame. She, knowing something about it, is suitably impressed.

Don't tell anybody! I spot a woman I knew only slightly, but liked, as she enters the room. Something about the way she's dressed, how she walks, her confidence – my gaydar kicks in; it doesn't often. Later I get chatting to her and drop some lesbian connection into the conversation. She comes out but immediately swears me to secrecy; I tell her not to worry.

You used to have sex with everyone didn't you? Some guy I don't recognise has just come up to me and said this. I turn to face him. I drawl *Oh... never more than twelve at a time.* I maintain blistering eye contact. I'm not sure whether I am freezing or burning his balls off but it's definitely one or the other. He shuffles away to effect repairs, head down.

People crossed the street to avoid me. Psychiatric nurse again when we meet up a couple of years later. She's talking about when she'd been pregnant with her second child. At forty. This one takes me a little longer. Shocked, I assure her I still enjoy sex.

I suppose people crossed the street to avoid me too.

I crossed two countries to avoid them.

Mercy

I love her. I'm a good sister.

I could smell it coming, I could taste it in the air. If I say it was metallic and salty, understand that tells you almost nothing. There is no language. Everything I'm saying is miles off. Imagine a distressed dolphin desperately trying to convey a complicated idea using body language while gazing up at you through murky green water, thick as soup. That's sort of where I am. I want you to understand so much. I'm struggling to find some way of explaining. I can tell you aren't getting it. But you will, you will.

The atmosphere was thrumming, nothing to see but it's like radiation, you don't see that, do you? It still strips you to the bone. My sister knew something bad was happening even if she didn't know what. There were words coming out of her mouth but I couldn't hear them. I needed everything I had to work out what to do next. When you hold the fate of the whole planet in your hands that's just the way it is.

I was doing the hard sums. Working out the chance of survival. And the cost. When the answer came it was clear. She'd be stretched out to a disc a few millimetres thick and, fully conscious, bounced up and down on an infinitely hot griddle, according to an eternal celestial rhythm, the stars nodding along complacently. Meanwhile, I'd be on my hands and knees being fucked up the arse by the Crab Nebula.

Earlier I had watched while all the o's in my father and sister's conversation came loose from their speech and bobbed around my sitting room, becoming more and more numerous. I knew something very wrong was happening but I had let this go too far, way beyond any call for help.

I had to save her from what was coming, so I did. Any decent person would have done the same. It only took a few minutes before she stopped struggling. What's that compared to an eternity of pain? Then you lot arrived, all hot white metal and blue flashing lights, and stopped me from saving anyone else. You're telling me it'll be different tomorrow when the medication kicks in, that we'll all be on the same page then.

I'm looking forward to that.

Things To Do on Daffodil Ward

Not seen you before. First timer, yeah? Here's a few pointers from an old lag.

Smoke That's about it. The most important thing. Not on the ward itself of course but in a huddle outside in the enclosure at the back. This happens often; there's nearly always a staff member who wants a fag. Have your tobacco and skins on you at all times so you are ready to join in whenever a smoke break is granted. You need to see the sky, to feel the breeze. End up smoking much more than you would at home. In your longer stays you will eventually be trusted to go out the front on your own. Some of your most persistent memories will be formed here as you stand looking over the car park, planning how you will end this torture. You will still smoke much more than you would at home.

Wait That's the other main thing. You're either waiting to get discharged (manic, my usual style) or to be in a position to kill yourself (depressed) - though this probably requires being discharged too. No-one's ever managed it on a ward I've been on anyway. As far as I know. You're also waiting for meal times. Meal times are the best time of the day. Especially when pastry is involved. The most disappointing meal is Sunday evening when you will be presented with a salad of stupefying lack of imagination - naked pieces of lettuce, tomato and cucumber accompanied by a lump of cheddar or a hardboiled egg (vegetarian options). Even though this happens every week so the catering staff can knock off early you will be disappointed each time. Also hungry later.

Keep a low profile Important to escape the attention of the nastiest staff. The ones who look at the patients like they are pieces of shit. You know you're a piece of shit but you don't want to be treated like one. Plus they are too. Takes one to know one.

Conceal what you are thinking If they know that suicide dominates your thoughts (depression) or that your reality is fundamentally different from theirs and terrifying (mania), they'll never let you out. And getting out is your primary short-term goal. Focus on preventing it becoming a longer-term goal. Fortunately none of the staff are remotely interested in what is going on in your head. This will only seem strange to you if you have never spent time on a psychiatric ward.

Deal with the fact that nothing you say will be believed Because you are a mental patient. Even when what you are saying is true and desperately needs to be heard. Imagine - on your third or fourth admission you know you have been taking your lithium religiously, entirely complying (they love that word) with your prescription. Yet it has not prevented you going somewhat (not mind-blowingly) manic. Manic enough to end up in hospital. But not so manic you can't speak or be understood. You beg them to test your lithium levels. You plead with them. They need to understand that lithium simply isn't working for you - as it doesn't for about half of those who take it. The nurse just smiles and repeats her mantra that your levels will be tested in a week or two when they will have 'stabilised'. Rage, weep, nothing will move her. It happened to me. Swallowing that rage, that grief, that injustice, was hard.

Avoid the patients you find most difficult They do your head in too. This includes the ones who never stop talking at you if you make eye contact, the ones who smell bad, the ones who want to tell you how terrible they feel or how they are not loonies like everyone else and shouldn't be there, the ones who look at you in a horrible way and the ones you are frightened of because their rage seems on a hair trigger. (There's considerable overlap between the last two.) There are plenty of patients who do not fall into any of these groups. Patients who you can feel confident sitting quietly with, patients who will pass only occasional remarks about the staff and the general shittiness of the set up. Patients who don't take the piss out of other patients.

Cope with friends and relatives visiting / not visiting Both are difficult. Early in your career as a mental patient, if you are like me, you will feel deeply ashamed. Later, if you work on it, this will become less of an issue. Also you get more used to it. As do your visitors. In the early days, if they are like my visitors, they will be horrified at the lack of things for you to do, the lack of any therapy beyond drugs, the fact that you never seem to see a doctor. They will deploy their non-mental-patient status and any middle-class privilege they hold in trying to change these things. You will know it is futile. Eventually they will realise this too. You are simply being kept in a holding pen. This is the reality you and they must adjust to. I didn't say it was easy.

A Hideous Failure to Intervene

The radiator is making the strangest noises. In fact it's doing a lot more than that; it's twisting time and space and feeding them through its coils. I sort of know that's impossible but at the same time I can see it actually happening. Which makes me feel a bit sick. And frightened.

Right next to this cramped stuffy room two nurses are guarding a door. I watch them carefully while making sure they don't notice me. I can see them categorising all the people who come in or try to go out, arranging them into a hierarchy. By watching them closely I come to understand the principles by which they sort and grade them. I can understand their world view. I can predict their decision making. I can see people as if through their eyes. What kind of monster have I become?

It's to do with vitality and aliveness and correctness as these two terrifyingly cold women understand those concepts. Dark skinned people are easy, they are quick to be diverted to the left. Older, tired or ill looking people may get a second glance, then they too are gone. People with large noses, curly hair, thicker – or thinner – lips than average may get a moment or two's consideration before the inevitable left leaning decision is made. The showers of course are on the left. Only the young, pale and bland with smooth hair that is blonde or at worst light brown pass further in to the ward.

The women seem to be quietly enjoying what they are doing; it's not just a tedious duty, there is some pleasure to be had in it. They exchange glances, the tiniest of nods, supercilious smiles. They are comrades, sharing a comfortable superiority. There is a properness about what is happening for them. They never disagree, always perfectly in tune. They have the knowledge, they have the authority, they are doing what they are supposed to be doing and all of this is satisfactory to them.

I imagine their only slight regret is the absence of any resistance. A little physical abuse would introduce a pleasant variety for them. However, nobody challenges their decisions. Either the people destined for the showers don't understand what is about to happen to them or they are so utterly demoralised by this point that they don't care much. I fail to intervene although I can see exactly what is happening. Instead I take care not to be seen. Again I disgust myself utterly, unspeakably. My cowardice. My complicity.

Later I will be offered food, medication, a smoking break. Later I will search hopelessly, again and again.

Search hopelessly for a way out of this horror, this living hell, this life. This life I surely don't deserve to live.

I'm Not Saying She Saved My Life But

There once was a woman who gave me back my body.

Then she gave me a lifetime's friendship, a love that stood by me in my most impossible and unbearable manifestations. When all I wanted was oblivion. When I tried repeatedly to make that happen. When I was blind to anyone's needs but my own desperate desire for death. When I was no more than a stone round her neck choking her, dragging her down, destroying her hope, her appetite for life, her appetite even for food. Her getting scrawnier even as I bloated on medications and three hospital meals a day. More weary, lined and anxious even as I blanked all concerns beyond the next cigarette.

I'm not saying she saved my life but if not for a bit of detective-work with a copy of the Yellow Pages lying near the landline in my sitting room it's possible the ambulance wouldn't have tracked me down to that Premier Inn in time. And then of course there was the kicking-in of my front door she had to organise after I'd taken an overdose hefty enough to leave me more or less out for the count for the next three days on the psych ward.

So yeah, I've been a barrel-load of laughs really.

Don't get me wrong here. She's no saint, no self-effacing martyr. Christ, no! I don't really understand why she stuck with me. She had a man who loved her and, eventually, three great kids. I followed them up north and found a place to live not five minutes' walk away so one interpretation would be that she just got unlucky with a stalker.

I don't think she'd agree with that. At least not now we're more than fifteen years clear of the worst of my shit. But I wouldn't dare speak for her – she doesn't take kindly to that.

I can speak for me though.

I got lucky.

Fingling the Snargle

In that moment I knew I was going to fingle the snargle. I don't know how many times it had been forbidden. I don't remember if it was the thirty-second or thirty-third repetition that did it. All I can tell you is that there came a point at which I snapped. A point at which my fury at being manipulated boiled over and crystallised into a pure, sharp desire. I would fingle that snargle. And I would live to tell the tale.

Obviously I can't write my plans down so I'm storing them in a section of my head They don't know about. Should I fail, gods forbid, I pray I will find a way to communicate them to another.

First, you must avoid the Goodnight Drink. I discovered this when a stomach bug resulted in its violent expulsion three nights running, something They failed to notice. In my darkest moments I cling to this - They make mistakes. It's obvious now our food is drugged - witness the manic energy with which we attack our impossible workloads. But it's the Goodnight Drink that keeps it all together. Keeps things sweet. For Them.

The changes began on the second night. I always sleep straight through, dreamless, wake up raring to go. But that morning I had strange half memories, meaningless phrases reverberating. I felt tired, the day was harder, but I kept my head down - drawing attention to oneself is dangerous here.

On the third morning I started to understand. I realised a soundtrack had been playing in my ears all night. My surroundings looked different. I could still make out the luxurious appointments of my apartment but they were flimsy, wavering, a semi-transparent layer over a different scene, paler but somehow more solid. It was disorientating but I kept my nerve. Kept my mouth shut. It helped that, oddly, there was something almost comforting about the blurry double image.

I'll never know how I made the connection between these changes and the Drink. But I did. Bless my mother, who I had somehow forgotten, for insisting I learned the family trade. My skills of distraction and misdirection were to serve me well. And over the next few days my world changed entirely.

You must stay awake half the night, learning from the soundtrack. That's how I found out the snargle being fingled is Their greatest fear. They repeat hypnotically that it is essential to the mission, that it guides us to the new world where we will all, finally, live in peace and prosperity. They have to let us service it; its radiation is deadly. Their single weak point is our only chance.

Because you have to sleep you will still be influenced by Their words, though to a lesser extent. Be grateful - you must navigate Their world convincingly. I needed the shadows of my apartment, the exclusive spa in which I while away my days, the charming bohemian cafe on Level 5 where I meet my well-heeled friends. I needed to half believe I was swimming lazy lengths as I sweated in the hot dark tangle of pipework. I needed to half believe I lay between high thread count sheets as I tossed and turned in the crowded dormitory where my fellow captives snored and farted their way through the night.

You will be torn between secrecy and the uncomfortable realisation that you need an accomplice. I cannot conceive of fingling the snargle alone. A machine cannot be misdirected like a human. Or if it can I never learned those skills.

But who to choose? How can you know who will react with fury when they know the truth and who with resignation and despair? Who will have the strength to navigate this bizarre life of two contradictory halves? Who can you trust and who will betray you, still clinging to the lie of redemption? There's nothing to be gained by observation - in their present condition everyone is perfectly interchangeable.

It was easy to ensure her Drink didn't stay down the first time. A strategically placed glass of salt water. But she wouldn't fall for that again. And I needed three nights clear before I could risk speech. It took all my street magician skills to doctor the Drink itself on the second evening. Impossible to repeat; that suspicious look still raises goosebumps. The following morning she looked disorientated. We work together so I kept an eye on her. She muddled through and, thank all the gods, no alarm was raised. Nearly there. Wherever there is.

On the third night I perform a substitution so audacious I can hardly believe it works. But it does. That night I practise my speech over and over again. Only when every word is committed to memory do I let myself drift off to the endlessly murmuring soundtrack.

The next day she gets it. At least I think so. Makes all the right noises - it's impossible to know for sure. I show her how to avoid the Drink and we agree to wait a few days while reality comes into a sharper focus for her. She's tough and clever, learns fast, I've chosen well.

Those few days crawl past like centuries but finally we are as ready as we will ever be. The snargle squats in its lead-lined lair, thousands of tiny lights flickering as it performs its calculations. We approach. Speed is everything. The defingler is obvious, a thick black cable, above it the only light, green, that does not flicker. My accomplice protects me, flinging herself across the thing's sensory panel while I rip out the cable.

Everything changes. The scene pixelates and falls away in a shower of tiny particles. I turn to find my mother standing beside me. Her eyes are wet but she is smiling.

She takes my arm and together we walk out of the psychiatric ward and back into town.

Acknowledgements

It's a cliché, but true, that there are too many people to mention. So many flash fiction writers and teachers who have provided generous opportunities to write, learn and collaborate online and in person. My wonderful writers' groups, past and present, where I learned to hone my creative skills through giving and receiving critical feedback. I think you all know who you are...

And all the people I love. All the people who make me so glad I stuck around to live this life. I think you all know who you are too...

Thank you.

Printed in Great Britain
by Amazon

37906963R00067